The Marshall Cavendish (

GREEN & PLEA

·WALKS

The Lakes and Waterways of Cumbria

MARSHALL CAVENDISH

First published in Great Britain in 1997 by
Marshall Cavendish Books, London
(a division of Marshall Cavendish Partworks Ltd).

ISBN 1-85435-878-2

British Library Cataloguing in Publication Data:
A catalogue record for this book is available from the British Library

Printed and bound in Italy

Some of this material has previously appeared in the
Marshall Cavendish partwork *Out and About*.

Picture Credits
Heather Angel page 24. Jeffrey Beazley page 5, 13, 16. J. Allan Cash page 9. Mary Evans Picture
Library page 8, 28, 36. Derek Forss page 17, 25, 41. Simon Fraser page 44. Hello and Van Ingen/
NHPA page 20. R. Orr / Aquila page 40. John Watney page 12, 21, 29, 32, 33, 37. All other pictures:
Marshall Cavendish Picture Library

Art Editor: Joyce Mason
Designer: Richard Shiner
Editor: Irena Hoare
Picture Researcher: Vimu Patel
Production: Joanna Wilson

CONTENTS

GREEN & PLEASANT
——— WALKS ———

The walks in *GREEN & PLEASANT WALKS* will give you ideas for walks near your own neighbourhood, as well as in other areas of Britain.

All the walks are devised around a theme, and range in length from about 2 to 9 miles (3.25 to 14.5km). They vary in difficulty from very easy to mildly strenuous, and since each walk is circular, you will always end up back at your starting point.

Background information is given for many of the walks, relating legends, pointing out interesting buildings, giving details about famous people who have lived in the area. There are occasional 'Nature Facts' panels, which highlight some of the things you might see in the landscape as you walk.

THE LAW OF TRESPASS

If you find a right of way barred, the law says you may remove the obstruction, or take a short detour.

If the path is blocked by a field of crops, you may walk along the line of the path through the crops in single file. However, in England and Wales, if you stray from the path you are trespassing, and could be sued for damages.

If you do find that your path has been obstructed in some way, report the matter to the local authority, who will take the necessary action to clear the route.

It is illegal for farmers to place a bull on its own in a field crossed by a right of way (unless the bull is not a recognized dairy breed), but if you come across a bull on its own in a field, find another way round – and if you feel sufficiently aggrieved, report the farmer.

USING MAPS

Although this book of *GREEN & PLEASANT WALKS* gives you all the information you need to enjoy your walks, it is useful to have a larger scale map to give you detailed information about

---

THE COUNTRY CODE

- Enjoy the countryside, and respect the life and work of its inhabitants
- Always guard against any risk of fire
- Fasten all gates
- Keep your dogs under close control
- Keep to public footpaths across farmland
- Use gates and stiles to cross fences, hedges etc

- Leave livestock, crops and machinery alone
- Take your litter home with you
- Help to keep all water clean and unpolluted
- Protect wildlife, plants and trees
- Take special care on country roads
- Do not make any unnecessary noise

LAKES AND WATERWAYS OF CUMBRIA

❶ Common and Shore
❷ An Elizabethan Topiary
❸ The Tarn and the Water
❹ Wasdale Head
❺ Borrowdale Valley

❻ Wordsworth Country
❼ Vale of Eden
❽ John Peel Country
❾ East and West of Eden
❿ Gills and Valleys

All walks featured in this book are plotted and numbered on the regional map below, and listed in the box (left).

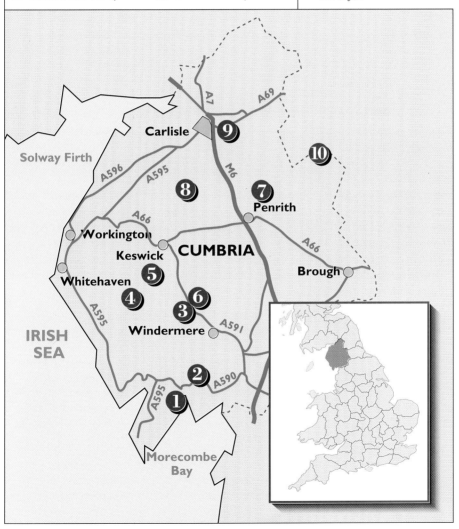

Lakes and Waterways of Cumbria

FACT FILE

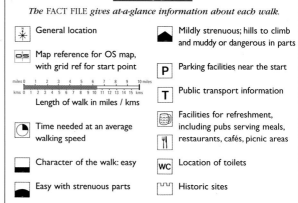

The FACT FILE gives at-a-glance information about each walk.

✳ General location	🏠 Mildly strenuous; hills to climb and muddy or dangerous in parts
OS Map reference for OS map, with grid ref for start point	P Parking facilities near the start
miles 0 1 2 3 4 5 6 7 8 9 10 miles kms 0 1 2 3 4 5 6 7 8 9 10 11 12 13 14 15 kms Length of walk in miles / kms	T Public transport information
🕐 Time needed at an average walking speed	🍴 Facilities for refreshment, including pubs serving meals, restaurants, cafés, picnic areas
▬ Character of the walk: easy	WC Location of toilets
◣ Easy with strenuous parts	🏰 Historic sites

GRID REFERENCES

All Ordnance Survey maps are over-printed with a framework of squares, called the National Grid. This is a reference system which, by breaking the country down into squares, lets you pinpoint an area and give it a unique number.

On OS Landranger, Pathfinder and Outdoor Leisure maps, a reference to an accuracy of 100m is possible. Grid squares on the maps cover an area of 1km x 1km on the ground.

GRID REFERENCES

Blenheim Palace, in Oxfordshire, has a grid reference of **SP 441 161**. This is constructed as follows:

SP: These letters identify the 100km grid square in which Blenheim Palace lies. The squares form the

basis of the National Grid. Information on the 100km square covering any given map is given in the map key.

441 161: This reference locates the position of Blenheim Palace to 100m in the 100km grid square.

44: This part of the reference is the number of the grid line which forms the western (left-hand) boundary of the 1km grid square in which Blenheim Palace appears. It is printed in the top and bottom margins of the relevant map (Pathfinder 1092 here).

16: This part of the reference is the number of the grid line which forms the southern boundary of the 1km grid square in which Blenheim Palace appears. The number is printed in the left and

right-hand margins of the relevant OS map (Pathfinder 1092 here).

Both numbers together (SP 4416) locate the bottom left-hand corner of the 1km grid square in which the Palace appears. The last figures in the reference **441 161** pinpoint the position in the square; dividing its western boundary lines into tenths and estimating on which imaginary tenths line the Palace lies.

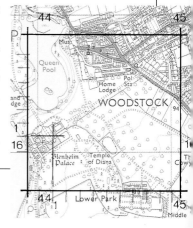

4

The Common and the Shore

The fascinating history and wildlife
of a corner of Furness

The walk follows the Ulverston Canal, passing beneath a railway bridge.

Ulverston is a lively market town, just inland from an inlet of Morecambe Bay. This circular walk explores its history, taking in a Bronze Age stone circle, several associations with the early days of the Quakers, and a rich industrial past.

It also passes through a variety of wildlife habitats, starting with the quiet willow-lined Ulverston Canal **Ⓐ**, now abandoned, which is a lovely stretch of water linking the town with the estuary. The path then skirts along the shore, where sandbanks are home to many wading birds, and eventually reaches a high limestone common, rich in flowers and plants. From here a footpath leads over the pretty Levy Beck, and back into town.

5

THE WALK

ULVERSTON–BARDSEA–BIRKRIGG COMMON
The walk begins at the brewery car park on the north side of Ulverston, just off the A590.

1 Turn left on A590. Beyond the Canal Tavern, turn right. Follow the canal **A** to its end, where there is a view of Leven Viaduct **B** to north. Cross canal, turn right down road.

2 At end of factory, fork left to Sea View Inn. Turn right, then left down narrow lane on left of post box. Cross Carter Beck, then go half left through gate along narrow path through field. Follow path as it bears right; continue south along field edge towards chimney **C**.

3 Just past chimney, climb stile and continue ahead along lane. Conishead Priory **D** is ahead, and Hermitage **E** is in trees on hill to right. Follow lane to beach. Turn right, along shore. Chapel Island is to left.

4 After crossing the second of two car parks, take right-hand stile of two; path through pasture to shore. At next car park, left down A5087; first right up to Bardsea **G**.

5 Turn left down lane past Braddyls Arms; left again down lane to Wellhouse; right at fork. Up to gate onto common.

6 Through gate, ahead short way. Turn left, cross track past stone circle **H**, to road. Turn right, continue through Sunbrick **J**. Small barrier in wall on left gives access to the Quaker burial ground **K**. Soon take path that strikes diagonally right to summit. Follow path slightly left, to road and turn right.

7 At crossroads, right again. Left after 500 yards (450m), through gate approached by grassy track. Take hedged track to road; turn right. After 50 yards (45m), left through gate by farm track.

8 Pass right of farm, to road. Just before first house on right, go through gate to alley. Through next gate to cross pasture to Croftlands Estate.

9 Bear left in front of Lancastrian pub, right on Mountbarrow Road. Opposite school, left on to Meeting House Lane. Continue over Urswick Road; bear left at Swarthmoor Hall **L**.

10 Just after the Hall, take path on right, to Springfield Road. At road, turn left; right into Conishead Road. Left under bridge, right into Brogden Street. At end, right onto A590; follow this to the roundabout **M**, and return to start.

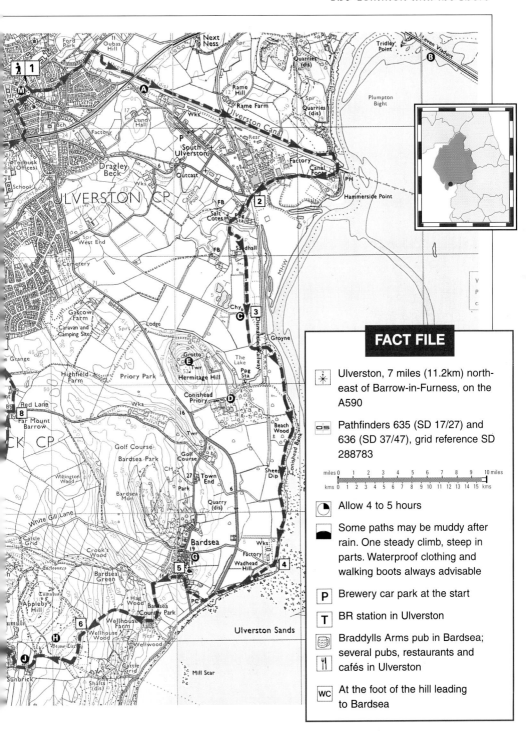

FACT FILE

Ulverston, 7 miles (11.2km) north-east of Barrow-in-Furness, on the A590

Pathfinders 635 (SD 17/27) and 636 (SD 37/47), grid reference SD 288783

miles 0 1 2 3 4 5 6 7 8 9 10 miles
kms 0 1 2 3 4 5 6 7 8 9 10 11 12 13 14 15 kms

Allow 4 to 5 hours

Some paths may be muddy after rain. One steady climb, steep in parts. Waterproof clothing and walking boots always advisable

P Brewery car park at the start

T BR station in Ulverston

Braddylls Arms pub in Bardsea; several pubs, restaurants and cafés in Ulverston

WC At the foot of the hill leading to Bardsea

The Quakers

George Fox, founder of the Society of Friends

George Fox was a charismatic Puritan preacher, born in 1624 in Leicestershire. From an early age, he roamed the Midlands and the North of England, proclaiming his belief that religious knowledge should come from an 'inner light' or God-given inspiration, rather than from the traditions of the established church.

Fox's message was welcomed in the North by, amongst others, a puritan sect called the Seekers. Men and women preachers, called Publishers of Truth, helped him to establish local congregations, particularly in Cumbria and Lancashire.

This group became the Society of Friends. They were called the Quakers, at first derisively, because they were said to tremble at the word of God.

The Quakers suffered persecution for denouncing the religious practices of the times. Fox himself was put into prison eight times between 1649 and 1673. The persecution was at its worst when the monarchy was restored to power in 1660.

When he was in Cumbria, Fox stayed at Swarthmoor Hall, the home of Judge Fell, a chancellor of the Duchy of Lancaster. Fell always made Fox welcome at the Hall, although he did not fully share the preacher's views. Fell died in 1658. His widow, Margaret, with whom he had eight children, converted to Quakerism and married Fox in 1669.

Fox died in 1691, less than two years after an Act of Toleration brought the persecution of the Quakers to an end.

An Elizabethan Topiary Garden

From Levens Hall along the route of the old Lancaster–Kendal canal

In the garden at Levens Hall, box and yew have been clipped into many shapes.

Levens Hall **Ⓐ**, where the walk starts, is an Elizabethan mansion house in the scenic countryside of southern Cumbria. The house is surrounded by its famous topiary garden, and across the road is Levens Deer Park, which has a Public Right of Way through it. The route winds through grasslands and woods of lime, beech, oak, ash and elm. The River Kent, turbulent in places, can be heard through the trees, and black fallow deer may be seen in the distance.

Beyond the park, a stone parapet gives a good view over a series of falls and a natural limestone salmon leap **Ⓒ**. The path goes past two old gunpowder mills, and through a pretty wood, before returning to Levens Hall and its famous avenue of oaks.

Lakes and Waterways of Cumbria

THE WALK

LEVENS BRIDGE–SEDGWICK

The walk begins outside the gates to Levens Hall ❶ at the gap stile on the north side of Levens Bridge, on the A6.

1 Cross stile, follow path through deer park for about ¾ mile (1.2km) to sign reading 'No exit beyond this point'. Bear left to steps up to stile in stone wall.

2 Turn sharp right and walk down beside a stone wall along the edge of the deer sanctuary ❷ through another stile in a stone wall. Keep straight ahead across the corner of a field to a third stile, which leads to a lane beside a house called Park Head.

3 Turn right, walk to end of lane, round walkway under A591 viaduct over River Kent, and past salmon leap ❸. On other side, walk up continuation of lane, beside river, to Force Bridge, where gunpowder mill ruins can be seen ❹.

4 Do not cross over Force Bridge, but continue straight along the lane, until arriving at a smaller lane on the right.

5 Turn right down this lane. Continue to suspension bridge on right, over river. On the way, lane on left leads to the 14th-century Sizergh Castle and gardens, owned by the National Trust.

6 If you continue past bridge, you enter private lane to caravan site in Low Park Wood. Beside this are remains of big gunpowder mill ❺. Permission to visit mill obtainable from caravan site office.

7 Retrace steps to the path, which crosses suspension bridge; turn left. Follow the river to Hawes Bridge and waterfall ❻. Ignore larger path that veers right. Several stiles/fences to climb.

8 At Hawes Bridge, turn right, along Natland Lane.

9 Before Crowpark Bridge, pass through small gate on left and turn right (south) down clearly defined path of dried-out canal, past Larkrigg Spring wood ❼, and continue, over stiles, to Sedgwick.

10 From aqueduct ❽ at Sedgwick, walk down steps into village, cross road and walk down road for Hincaster. At junction with road from Force Bridge, continue to left and cross the bridge over A591. Turn right into the lay-by among trees just beyond the bridge.

11 Cross the gap stile in the stone wall at the bottom of the lay-by and walk down the centre of the oak avenue ❾ all the way to stile at the end of the park. Cross the stile on to the A6 and cross this road for Levens Hall car park, or turn right over the bridge to the start of the walk.

10

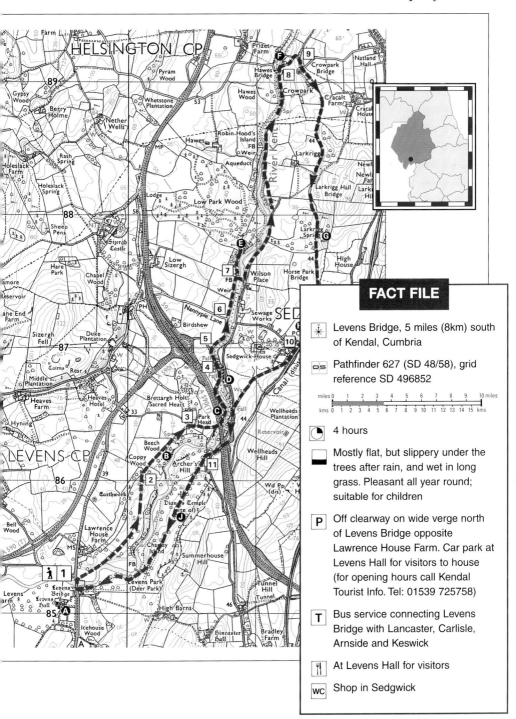

Levens Bridge, 5 miles (8km) south of Kendal, Cumbria

Pathfinder 627 (SD 48/58), grid reference SD 496852

miles 0 1 2 3 4 5 6 7 8 9 10 miles
kms 0 1 2 3 4 5 6 7 8 9 10 11 12 13 14 15 kms

4 hours

Mostly flat, but slippery under the trees after rain, and wet in long grass. Pleasant all year round; suitable for children

P Off clearway on wide verge north of Levens Bridge opposite Lawrence House Farm. Car park at Levens Hall for visitors to house (for opening hours call Kendal Tourist Info. Tel: 01539 725758)

T Bus service connecting Levens Bridge with Lancaster, Carlisle, Arnside and Keswick

⑂⑂ At Levens Hall for visitors

WC Shop in Sedgwick

A History of Danger

Ruins of Sedgwick gunpowder mill. Gunpowder was milled for about 600 years until the mid-19th century, when nitroglycerine was discovered.

Gunpowder was first manufactured in Cumbria in 1764. Before this it had been made mainly in the south, and was used mostly for military purposes, for propelling missiles. As the mining industry grew in Cumbria, a coarser gunpowder, from a local source, was urgently needed for blasting in the mines.

It was John Wakefield (1738–1811), a local Quaker, who had the idea of harnessing the power of the swift waters of the River Kent to grind gunpowder for mining use. In 1790, he built a mill at Force Bridge, the ruins of which can still be seen from the bank of the river.

Gunpowder in its simplest form is a mixture of saltpetre, sulphur and charcoal, ground to a powder. In this state it ignites rapidly and, if confined, its combustion acts as an explosive.

In the 18th century no material that might set off an explosion was allowed near a gunpowder mill, but despite this accidents were common, and gunpowder milling was a very hazardous industry.

The last gunpowder mill in Cumbria was closed in 1937.

The Tarn and the Water

A short walk that visits two very different lakes

The jagged Langdale Pikes form a backdrop to the view across the Loughrigg Tarn.

The village of Elterwater **Ⓐ**, a cluster of stone houses at the foot of the Langdale Pikes, grew up around the bridge over the Great Langdale Beck. This was carefully sited where the solid rock of the gorge upstream gives way to the peaty mud at the fringes of the lake. Just upstream from the bridge are the remnants of a waterwheel. The mill it powered once produced gunpowder for use in the Lakeland mines and quarries.

The sheared, slaty rocks that form the rugged scenery in this part of the Lake District were formed from ancient lava and volcanic ash, and are known geologically as the Borrowdale Volcanic Series. The stone is almost as hard as flint, and was used by Stone Age man to make axes.

Continued on p. 16➡

13

THE WALK

ELTERWATER–SKELWITH BRIDGE
The walk begins at Elterwater Common.

1 Walk up the lane through Elterwater **A** to the B5343. Turn right. Turn first left by a signposted boulder, and follow the lane, past some woods and a road joining from the right, until you reach T-junction.

2 Turn right along the lane for almost 200 yards (180m), then turn left over a wooden stile by a wooden gate. Go ahead, then bear right and cross a wooden step stile over the stone wall, with Loughrigg Tarn **B** on your right. Follow the path up a grassy slope to a lane at the top. Go through a wooden gate and turn right along the stony lane.

3 Go through the wooden gate at the end of the lane and turn right down the lane that crosses it. Follow this lane as it bends left down to a road. Turn right.

4 After crossing a little stream, turn left down another lane. Follow it downhill to a main road.

5 Cross the road on your right, and walk past the Skelwith Bridge Hotel towards Skelwith Bridge **C**. Before the bridge, turn right towards the Kirkstone Green Slate Quarry Company, with the river on your left. In front of the slate shop, turn right and then left around the building and through the slate works. Continue ahead, along the woodland path, with the river still on your left. In a short while you will pass Skelwith Force **D**. Continue along the lane to its end.

6 Go through a gate into a field. Follow a distinct grassy path the length of the field to the head of Elter Water **E**. Go through a kissing-gate and follow the path, which goes through woodland then back into Elterwater village.

Nature Facts

Winter

Summer

Black-necked grebe. This bird normally visits Britain in winter.

Summer

Winter

Black-throated diver. These birds breed on inland lakes.

Summer

Red-throated diver. You may see these birds' nests near small lakes.

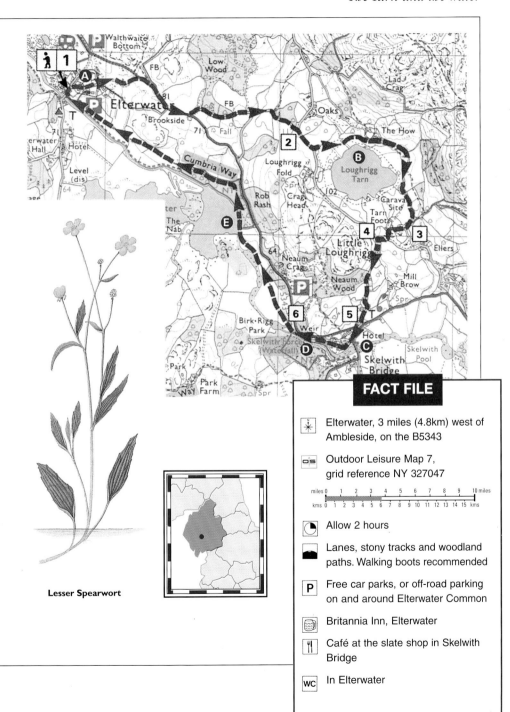

Lesser Spearwort

FACT FILE

Elterwater, 3 miles (4.8km) west of Ambleside, on the B5343

Outdoor Leisure Map 7, grid reference NY 327047

miles 0 1 2 3 4 5 6 7 8 9 10 miles
kms 0 1 2 3 4 5 6 7 8 9 10 11 12 13 14 15 kms

Allow 2 hours

Lanes, stony tracks and woodland paths. Walking boots recommended

Free car parks, or off-road parking on and around Elterwater Common

Britannia Inn, Elterwater

Café at the slate shop in Skelwith Bridge

In Elterwater

Today, it is used everywhere in the roofs and walls of buildings, and in the dry-stone walling that defines the boundaries here. It also offers shelter for the Herdwick sheep that graze the slopes.

The first part of the route leads along quiet lanes towards Loughrigg Tarn **B**. This is as attractive now as it was back in 1810, when William Wordsworth described it in his famous *Guide to the Lakes* as "a most beautiful example of a miniature lake, a small, quiet and fertile domain, with a margin of green firm meadows, surrounded by rocky and barren steeps, overlooked by the solemn pikes of Langdale".

Long Views

On the uphill stretch to the lake, it is worth pausing to take in the view south-west of the Old Man of Coniston; Wetherlam is the nearest, then Swirl How and Grey Friar. The jagged Langdale Pikes stand out to the west. A lane leads to the Langdale road at Skelwith Bridge **C**, which crosses the River Brathay. The river once formed the boundary between Westmorland and Lancashire.

Just before the bridge are the shop and workshop of the Kirkstone Slate Company. The attractive local green slate-stone is made from volcanic ash laid down in thin layers that split easily, like slate. It is used all over the world for making fireplaces and for facing buildings.

The volcanic rocks are very resistant to erosion by water or ice, and a bar of this rock has formed a waterfall, Skelwith Force **D**, where the River Brathay cascades into deep, greenish pools. The falls are especially impressive after rain.

Downstream from here, the Brathay flows gently over sand, silt and clay washed from the upper valleys. It runs into a saucer-shaped hollow, scoured out of the softer rock by ancient glaciers, and now filled with the still waters of Elter Water **E**. The lake is slowly getting smaller; at one time, the flat land around the Water was a part of the lake. Gradually, however, reeds have colonized the sediment on its fringes, a process which is still continuing.

The River Brathay tumbles over the rocks at Skelwith Force, on its way to Elter Water.

The path goes through a National Trust woodland, where oak, ash, larch, birch and beech trees can be found. Willows and alders grow by the Water, and on it float nut-like alder seeds. From here, the route returns to the village of Elterwater, along the Langdale Beck.

Wasdale Head

Through mountains high above the deepest lake in England

The pyramid-shaped Great Gable rises 2,949 feet (900m) above Wast Water.

Wast Water is England's deepest lake — at 258 feet (79m) below the surface, its bed is actually lower than sea level. Driving towards Wasdale Head, the first view is across the lake to the great crumbling scree slopes, 2,000 feet (610m) high, which have been slowly slipping into the lake since a glacier undercut the fellside thousands of years ago. Fingers of the ice-age glacier also scoured out the deep grooves of Mosedale, Styhead and Lingmell, closing in at Wasdale Head.

On this short, low-level walk around Wasdale Head, you are surrounded by the dramatic crags of Yewbarrow, Great Gable, Kirk Fell, and Scafell Pike, which at 3,206 feet (980m) is the highest point in

Continued on p. 20➔

17

THE WALK

WASDALE HEAD

The walk begins from the Green at the end of the Wasdale Head road.

1 From the Green, walk back a little distance along the road towards the lake.

2 Cross the small bridge–'Down in the Dale Bridge'–then turn right, and go through the kissing gate in the fence on the right. Walk forward along a grassy path which runs above the Mosedale Beck, from where there are good views ❶ of Great Gable. Continue along this path, which becomes stonier, crossing two little becks and going through a gate, until you are opposite the Wasdale Head Hotel on the far bank.

3 Continue left along the broad stony track between drystone walls. Pass through a kissing gate, next to a five-barred gate (marked 'Waterfalls and Ritson's Force'). Continue on upwards along the grassy

path, which follows a wall on the right. From here, there are good views back, with drystone walls showing the medieval field patterns ❷ of Wasdale Head.

4 By a solitary larch tree turn right, passing between the end of a stone wall and a wire fence. Cross the stony, mossy area through the copse of larch trees, down to Ritson's Force ❸, which is a series of small waterfalls on the Mosedale Beck (care needed above the rocky gorge). Return by the same route to Stage 3 opposite the Hotel.

5 Cross over Row Bridge ❹, a small, picturesque packhorse bridge, and turn left to walk along the broad, stony track that runs beside the beck. The path crosses over another little beck and begins to rise.

6 Watch for a smaller path that forks to the right. Take this path, following another beck (Fogmire Beck). Cross over the beck (right) by a plank bridge. Cross and recross the same beck by three more bridges, until you come to a wooden gate. Go through, cross yet another bridge, and walk on between stone walls towards some farm buildings.

7 Follow the barn wall to the left, then go through the gate on the right into the farmyard of Burnthwaite. Walk through the farmyard, join the track, and turn right to leave Burnthwaite. Continue along the track until you come to the tiny church ❺ among the yew trees.

8 After you have seen the church, rejoin the track and continue on to where the walk started.

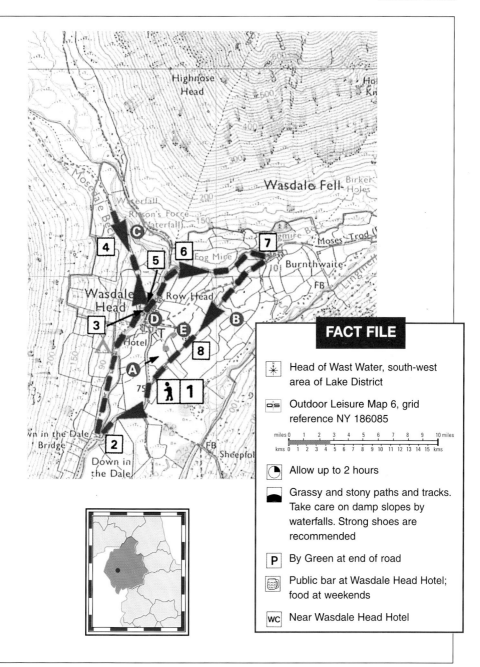

FACT FILE

✳	Head of Wast Water, south-west area of Lake District
os	Outdoor Leisure Map 6, grid reference NY 186085

miles 0　1　2　3　4　5　6　7　8　9　10 miles
kms 0　1　2　3　4　5　6　7　8　9　10　11　12　13　14　15　kms

🕐	Allow up to 2 hours
▬	Grassy and stony paths and tracks. Take care on damp slopes by waterfalls. Strong shoes are recommended
P	By Green at end of road
🍺	Public bar at Wasdale Head Hotel; food at weekends
WC	Near Wasdale Head Hotel

19

England. After walking a little distance towards the lake, you join a path parallel to the Mosedale beck, at the foot of Yewbarrow. The grassy slopes provide sparse grazing for Herdwick sheep.

Formidable Crags

There are good views ❶ of Great Gable and Kirk Fell, formed from a great dome of Borrowdale volcanic rock. Great Gable is an imposing, pyramid-shaped mountain. At 2,949 feet (900m) high it stands apart from the surrounding ranges, and its formidable crags have made it one of the most rewarding peaks for climbers. The rock faces below the summit include such named ascents as Napes Needle, the Innominate Crack, the Kern Knotts Crack, and Eagle's Nest Ridge.

A left turn between dry stone walls takes you into Mosedale. After a short climb uphill, there is a good view back to Wasdale Head, showing the pattern of fields ❷ bounded by drystone walls. A liberal scattering of boulders from the nearby fells was an invitation to the medieval settlers to use them for buildings and to enclose fields.

The fields' patterns are a clue to their age. Early field systems were small and irregular in shape, and the boundary walls

Teal, which are typical 'dabbling' ducks, are the smallest ducks in Britain.

meandered around natural obstacles. These old walls often trace corners in a curve instead of a right angle.

After the Enclosure Acts, maps were marked out geometrically, making it easier to calculate the area to be allotted to each person. The walls were then built with great precision.

Further uphill, there is a copse of larch trees and the way leads down to a grassy bank by the Mosedale Beck, where there is a series of little waterfalls known as Ritson's Force ❸. The shady copse is spongy with cushions of moss, including sphagnum moss, well-known to gardeners.

The trees and the tumbled stones of an old building are thickly covered with lichens, which are responsive to air quality, and thrive here, where the air is very pure.

Returning downhill to cross the picturesque packhorse bridge ❹, you now follow the beck towards Burnthwaite Farm. The track from Burnthwaite leads past the church ❺, amongst yew trees.

Climbing first became popular at the beginning of this century, and there are memorials at the church to those who have died on the mountains. On Great Gable there is a plaque dedicated to climbers who died fighting in World War I.

20

The Borrowdale Valley

A walk through wetland with breathtaking views

From Lingy End, there is a fine view of the 1,640-foot (500-m) Eagle Crag.

The Borrowdale valley has long been known as an area of great beauty. The novelist Hugh Walpole chose it as the setting for his saga *The Herries Chronicle.*

Walpole owned Brackenburn, a house overlooking Derwentwater, at Manesty, near Rosthwaite. The fictional site of the house where his hero, Rogue Herries, supposedly lived is said to be near where Hazel Bank Hotel **B** stands. A house at Watendlath **D**, may have been the model for the home of his heroine, Judith Paris.

Castle Crag is visible to the west as you walk, and from the hills there are views of the 'Jaws of Borrowdale'. The path climbs to lonely Dock Tarn, then falls steeply into the valley and back to the start.

THE WALK

ROSTHWAITE–WATENDLATH
The walk begins at the small car park on
the edge of Rosthwaite village.

1 From car park go to main road; left at road; right at sign to Stonethwaite/Watendlath. Cross bridge. Where track divides, go left. Follow path up, Hazel Bank Hotel **B** on right. Through private wood, on raised path. Through gate, path turns right, then left at stream on right, climbs upwards. Land is open, with trees. At gate is view **C** of 'Jaws of Borrowdale'. Path goes over open ground to gate.

2 Go through gate, with stream left. In 300 yards (275m) stream crosses under and continues right of path, which gets steep and rocky. Ignore gate in wall, with sign to Bowderstone and Keswick. Continue up, through another gate. After 200 yards (180m), with plantations right, path starts to descend; Watendlath in view. At bottom, go through gate,

over bridge, to hamlet **D**.

3 Leave Watendlath; cross bridge, and go through gate, but do not take path up hill. Instead fork left, take walled track beside Tarn; pass through two gates and cross small stream that runs across track. Cross another stream flowing across path; bear right, following arrow, with stream on right. Path is rocky, goes uphill to gate, beyond which is notice asking walkers to preserve wetland. Here path is marked by posts with blue/green tops. Where paths join, keep left; follow marker posts, over stepping stones. After gentle climb, ground becomes level but can be wet. Cross stream across path, through gate. Next part very steep with steps; then levels, rocks right; leads to Dock Tarn **E**.

4 At far end of Tarn path swings right and loses height, with

stream on left. Soon, Eagle Crag and Langstrath valley can be seen in front and to left. Climb stile over wall; views of Greenup Gill on left. Also views at ruined building **F**.

5 Path falls steeply, with steps, to valley. Stream appears left; cross stile. Soon wood ends, ground slopes away. Wall to right. At broad track, turn right, with wall left. Go through gate, continue on (avoid left turn through gate to Stonethwaite). Track here is part of 'Cumbria Way'. Nearly 1/2 mile (800m) from Stonethwaite, after many twists, path meets bend in Stonethwaite Beck, forming pool.

6 After more turns, path straightens, and follows beck to junction of paths below hotel. Left across bridge, left along road; right before post office to return to car park.

22

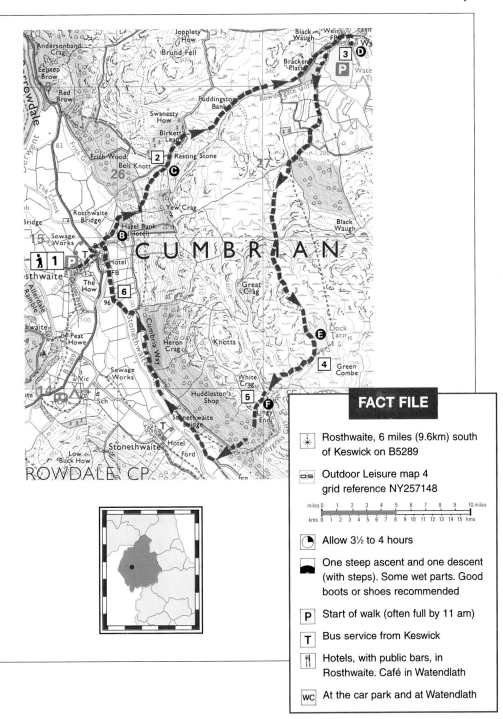

FACT FILE

✳	Rosthwaite, 6 miles (9.6km) south of Keswick on B5289
OS	Outdoor Leisure map 4 grid reference NY257148

miles 0 1 2 3 4 5 6 7 8 9 10 miles
kms 0 1 2 3 4 5 6 7 8 9 10 11 12 13 14 15 kms

◐	Allow 3½ to 4 hours
⬛	One steep ascent and one descent (with steps). Some wet parts. Good boots or shoes recommended
P	Start of walk (often full by 11 am)
T	Bus service from Keswick
¶	Hotels, with public bars, in Rosthwaite. Café in Watendlath
WC	At the car park and at Watendlath

Borrowdale's Ferns

The parsley fern, seen here in its spring growth, also grows in the Alps and the far North.

Like most of the flowering plants of Britain, ferns have roots that draw nutrients and water out of the soil, a system of veins through which these nutrients are distributed and leafy shoots of new growth. However, they do not produce fruits or flowers. Instead, they use spores as their means of reproduction.

The climate around Borrowdale is an extremely damp one – the village of Seathwaite, 2 miles (3.2km) away, is the wettest inhabited place in England, with 126 inches (320cm) of rain a year – and this suits ferns very well. At least twelve different species can be seen on this walk.

Maidenhair spleenwort grows in Rosthwaite on a wall by the car park, and also on the sides of the bridge.

Wall rue and rustyback grow on the garden walls of the house next to Rosthwaite's post office. Golden-scaled male fern is abundant high on the hillside behind the Hazel Bank Hotel, and grows beside the path in many places. Hard fern and lemon-scented fern also grow here.

Perhaps the best part of the walk if you are looking for ferns is the enclosed walled track that skirts Watendlath Tarn and beyond – polypody, male fern, lady fern, beech fern and lemon-scented fern can all be found growing in abundance. There is also bracken, which is widespread on the route, as well as the delicate parsley fern, so typical of Lakeland rocks and walls, and often used by gardeners in rockeries.

Where Wordsworth Wrote

Along the coffin road between two of Wordsworth's homes

It is easy to see how Rydal Water, shrouded in mist, would conjure poetic imagery.

The arch of Pelter Bridge provides an elegant start to the walk. Leaving the road, you come to the Church of St. Mary **A**, whose site was selected by Wordsworth. Opposite the church entrance, a gate leads to Dora's Field **B**, which Wordsworth planted with daffodils for his daughter. It is overgrown, but still pretty in spring. The poet's best known poem, of course, is 'Daffodils' ('I wandered lonely as a cloud...'), of 1804.

Up the road is Rydal Mount **C**, where Wordsworth lived for 37 years. The path follows the 'coffin road', once used for funeral processions, and skirts Rydal Water on its way to Dove Cottage, where the poet lived from 1799 to 1808. You return through woodland to the start of the walk.

THE WALK

RYDAL–DOVE COTTAGE

Head north on the A591, turn left before Rydal, over stone arch of Pelter Bridge. Turn right, cross a cattle grid and continue to car park, where the walk starts.

1 Retrace steps, turn left over Pelter Bridge. Follow pavement until pavement appears on opposite side; cross, continue to lane on right, signed 'Rydal Mount'. Pass church **A** and entrance to Dora's field **B**, left. Steep section of lane passes Rydal Mount **C** on left. Above this is lane to left signposted to Grasmere.

2 Follow lane (the 'coffin road') through two gates, before emerging from between walls onto fellside. Continue on track, passing through wall via a wooden gate, then a gap in next wall (no gate). Keep on past block of stone (Coffin Rest Stone **D**) on right, then through gate. Track splits. Take lower path, dipping slightly, then rising to follow wall on left. Lane dips to cross stream. Soon pass small gate and overgrown lane to left, Brockstone House to right.

3 Continue along coffin road, cross beck, path becomes surfaced road. Past White Moss Pond **E** on right, steep descent to junction.

4 Bear right down lane short way to Dove Cottage **F**. Retrace steps to junction, turn right. Road goes to Rydal Water, joining A591 by White Moss Common **G**.

5 Bear left in car park to emerge at main entrance. Cross main road, go through break in wall; steps lead down to flat area by the River Rothay.

6 Bear right on track (river directly in front), cross bridge over river. Continue through woods; track gets steeper and emerges through gate onto lane and open fells.

7 Take path opposite, which leads across flanks of fell, to larger path, horizontal along fellside (Loughrigg Terrace). Bear left; fine views across Rydal Water to Nab Cottage **H**. Path rises to top of knoll, then dips to cross levelled embankment. Huge cavern in hill, right, is Rydal Cave **J**.

8 Track twists down and passes quarry, right, then levels. Reaches open ground above lake.

9 Descend left, follow steep path across lakeside track that rises from shore. Pass through gate at edge of Jobson Close. Follow through woods to gate at their end. Path crosses open field to wooden gate or stile. Cross bridge over River Rothay, turn right along pavement by A591. Badger Bar is opposite.

10 Follow pavement through Rydal, back to Pelter Bridge and car park at start of walk.

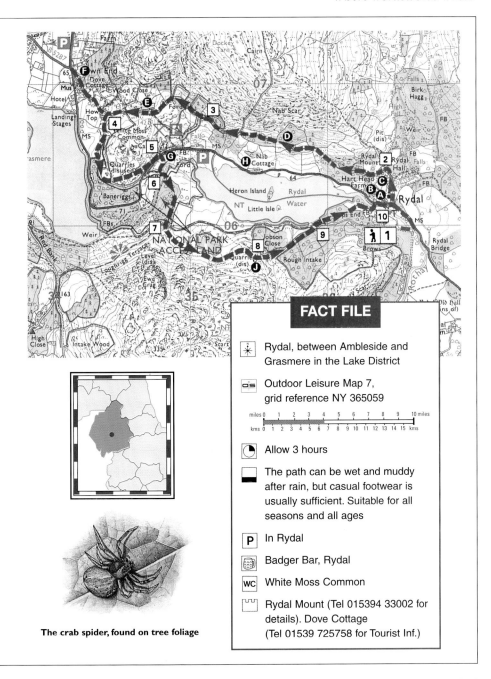

The crab spider, found on tree foliage

FACT FILE

☀ Rydal, between Ambleside and Grasmere in the Lake District

🅾🆂 Outdoor Leisure Map 7, grid reference NY 365059

miles 0 1 2 3 4 5 6 7 8 9 10 miles
kms 0 1 2 3 4 5 6 7 8 9 10 11 12 13 14 15 kms

◔ Allow 3 hours

▬ The path can be wet and muddy after rain, but casual footwear is usually sufficient. Suitable for all seasons and all ages

P In Rydal

🍺 Badger Bar, Rydal

WC White Moss Common

⌂ Rydal Mount (Tel 015394 33002 for details). Dove Cottage (Tel 01539 725758 for Tourist Inf.)

William Wordsworth

*Across the years, Wordsworth has meant different things to different people.
This caricature is by Sir Max Beerbohm.*

Inspired by the countryside of the Lake District, the poems of William Wordsworth broke with the conventional structure and stylized imagery of his day, and eloquently described the wild, natural beauty of the Lakes. From his relatively simple, and therefore unforgettable, poem 'Daffodils' to the masterly 'Ode on Intimations of Immortality', the poet explored the worlds of nature and human emotion in a new poetic language.

Wordsworth was born on 7 April 1770, in Cockermouth, on the edge of the Lake District. He was the son of an attorney, and was educated at Hawkshead Grammar School, where he first wrote poetry, and at St John's College, Cambridge.

For a while, he lived in the West Country and, with the help of a legacy, set up home with his sister, Dorothy. It was here that he first met Samuel Taylor Coleridge.

In 1799, after a period of travel, he and Dorothy moved into Dove Cottage, Grasmere, where he wrote much of his best work. He married Mary Hutchinson in 1802. In 1808, with a fourth child on the way, he and his family moved to rented accommodation in Grasmere, and five less happy years followed. In 1813, they moved to Rydal Mount, where Wordsworth spent his last years. He was made Poet Laureate in 1843 and died on 23 April 1850.

Wordsworth dearly loved the Lake District, and his *Guide to the Lakes*, written in 1810, is a much-acclaimed tourist guidebook, which remains a best-seller to this day.

The Vale of Eden

Through unspoilt countryside in north-east Cumbria

Lacy's caves are carved into a Gothic-style folly.

Far away from the tourist areas of Cumbria, yet with clear views of the Lakeland mountains and the highest part of the Pennines, lies the Vale of Eden. This walk leads through the valley and encompasses two quiet sandstone villages, the River Eden, industrial archaeology, a rich man's folly and one of the largest Megalithic sites in Britain.

Little Salkeld **A** is a red sandstone village, with a 19th-century Hall largely concealed behind ivy-clad walls. More accessible is the working water mill **G**, which you can visit by appointment. There is a mill shop selling organic flour, oats and oatmeal.

To the west of the village runs the Carlisle–Settle railway, opened in 1876. Part of the route is very close to the line,

Continued on p.32 ➤

29

THE WALK

LITTLE SALKELD–GLASSONBY
The walk begins at the triangular village green in Little Salkeld **A**.

1 Park on a side roads off the green. Take right fork past end wall of Salkeld Hall into a farm road, by a sign 'Private. No unauthorised vehicles Public Footpath Only'.

2 Walk full length of private road beside railway line until stopped by a road barrier and sign 'PRIVATE Long Meg'.

3 Turn sharp left down track to 'Lacy's Caves and Daleraven', beside an electricity sub-station. Follow path between wire fences across site of railway sidings **B** and on into trees opposite railway viaduct **C**. Continue past remains of mine workings on your right. The weir is on your left.

4 Shortly after passing weir, look for very small, overgrown path to remains of turbine house beside weir. Avoid this path when ground is wet and slippery and take care with young children. Follow original path to go through wood, beside river, to Lacy's Caves.

5 At point where path climbs up over cliff, take narrow path to left to first of Lacy's Caves. Avoid walking round outside of entrance, as narrow sandstone ledge is slippery when damp, and water is deep and fast-flowing below.

6 Retrace steps to main path. Climb over top of cliff and walk down through plantation, across pastures to gate to road by Daleraven Bridge.

7 On the road, turn right and walk up the 3/4-mile (1,200-m) road to Glassonby **E**.

8 In Glassonby, keep to right round tiny green; follow signposted road to Little Salkeld, passing forge on right (blacksmith not there full-time). After Glassonby Hall (large house with enclosed courtyard) and another house, continue for 200 yards (180m), then turn right by barn up a track to church of St Michael.

9 At rear of church-yard follow path out of gate, over field. Cross farm road, then cross fields, with wall on right. Pass through two gates, to field where Long Meg and her Daughters **F** stand.

10 Leave stones, take same path, which becomes a lane. Left at first junction, carry on to crossroads on Glassonby-Little Salkeld road. Right for short walk to green (pub marked on map not licensed). The Mill **G** is south of village, by bridge over Little Gill.

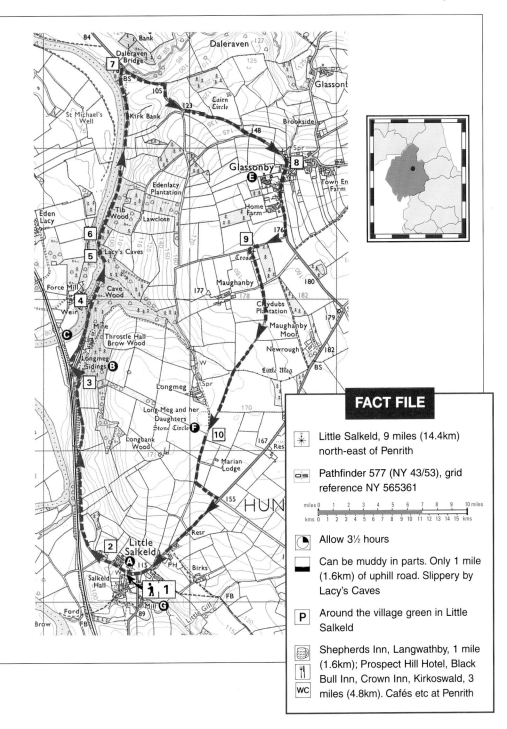

FACT FILE

Little Salkeld, 9 miles (14.4km) north-east of Penrith

Pathfinder 577 (NY 43/53), grid reference NY 565361

miles 0 1 2 3 4 5 6 7 8 9 10 miles
kms 0 1 2 3 4 5 6 7 8 9 10 11 12 13 14 15 kms

Allow 3½ hours

Can be muddy in parts. Only 1 mile (1.6km) of uphill road. Slippery by Lacy's Caves

P Around the village green in Little Salkeld

Shepherds Inn, Langwathby, 1 mile (1.6km); Prospect Hill Hotel, Black Bull Inn, Crown Inn, Kirkoswald, 3 miles (4.8km). Cafés etc at Penrith

so there is a chance of a close-up view of an old-fashioned steam train on its way to or from Carlisle.

The walk goes through what were the sidings **❸** of the Long Meg gypsum and anhydrite mine. Gypsum is used to make plaster of Paris and plasterboard, anhydrite for making sulphuric acid. There are rusting notices, which will interest railway buffs. Today, photographers cross the silent sidings to take close-up shots of the steam trains.

The path follows the track of a long-gone mine tramway, perched on a ledge with a steep, wooded drop down to sheep meadows on one side. A rock escarpment rises on the other side. To the left the railway line curves away towards Carlisle over a spectacular viaduct **❸**, 137 feet (41m) long and 60 feet (18m) high, which spans a curved broad reach of the Eden, and which took four years to build.

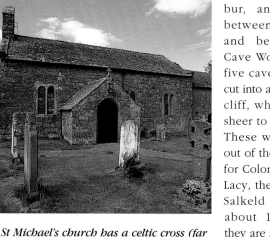

St Michael's church has a celtic cross (far right) in the churchyard.

Past Power
On the right of the path the rock face is shored up with ancient timbers and there are vestiges of inclined planes and unloading bays for the tubs which came down from the mines to the tramway in the last century: this is industrial archaeology at its best. From the river comes the sound of roaring water where it bubbles over a wide, rock-strewn weir. Half-submerged in the water are the ruins of a substantial turbine house, which produced electricity to augment the steam power used in the mines and plaster works above. An old corn mill stands opposite.

The way continues to follow the river bank, which is colourful with Himalayan balsam and butterbur, and passes between the oaks and beeches of Cave Wood. Then five caves appear, cut into a sandstone cliff, which drops sheer to the water. These were hewn out of the soft rock for Colonel Samuel Lacy, the owner of Salkeld Hall, in about 1867, and they are still named after him. Some say that Lacy's caves were wine cellars, others say he employed a man to live there as a hermit.

The path gets steep as it climbs to the sleepy village of Glassonby **❸**, with St Michael's church, whose origins go back to Saxon times, nearby. It takes you on to the stone circle known as Long Meg and her Daughters **❸**, built about 1750 BC, and from here you return to Little Salkeld.

John Peel Country

A riverside walk below the northern fells of Cumbria

Thick woodland grows around tumbling Whelpo Beck, above the Howk gorge.

Hesket Newmarket **A** was a flourishing market town in the 18th century and the home of many of the miners who worked in the surrounding hills. The route leads along a high path above the River Caldew until it joins the Cald Beck at Waters Meet **C**. This is a tranquil spot in the setting of a small wood made almost an island by the river's meandering curves and the Cald Beck that flows into it. During dry spells this stretch of river disappears down swilly holes, and you can walk beside the river bed to search for fossils. Here you may follow the path through Parson's Park, or follow the beck. Both ways lead to Caldbeck village **D**, where John Peel's gravestone can be seen in St Kentigern's church graveyard.

THE WALK

HESKET NEWMARKET–CALDBECK
The walk starts at the kissing gate across the village green
opposite the Old Crown **B** in Hesket Newmarket **A**.

1 Follow stream to bridge, through gate.

2 Turn right; follow slope, through gate; left by fence, to beck. Go through trees, gates, along beck, then river. Slope eases, flat ground by river until way is blocked.

3 Gate to field. Aim for corner of wire fencing ahead; diagonally over field, left; aim for two trees, high ground.

4 At trees go right past post; through gate to trees. Down steps, path through trees; gate to field.

5 Follow right-hand curve of grass ridge to gate/stile, edge of wood. Cald Beck on one side, Caldew on other.

6 Into wood over stile; keep sound of water both sides; to where waters meet **C**. Back to gate.

7 Cross bridge. Ahead for path to Caldbeck, or stay by beck (track over meadows) to bridge. Do not cross.

8 To right, low point in fence by ruin. Red paint and 'G' indicate step/stone. Through wire; left on path at bottom of slope.

9 Stile; open ground; road to village; bridge; gate to church **E**.

10 Leave by east gate; lane to Mill **F**. Road to Wigton.

11 Left in car park; right, then left along lane, before pond. .

12 Ahead to door with sign 'To Howk'. Cross yard; path to bobbin mill **G**. Steps through Howk **H**; bridge.

13 To shorten walk cross bridge to

field, then over stile at far side to road outside village. Or take path along beck to Whelpo Bridge.

14 Cross bridge; walk south side of beck to a school.

15 On right, at start of cottages, sign for 'Cumbria Way'. Continue to weir. Cross bridge, up bank to stile to field. If clear, aim for High Pike. Otherwise follow powerlines across field; cross wall. Left to farm. Stile north of buildings. Keeping close to hedges, cross fields / three stiles to steps in wall. Right to start.

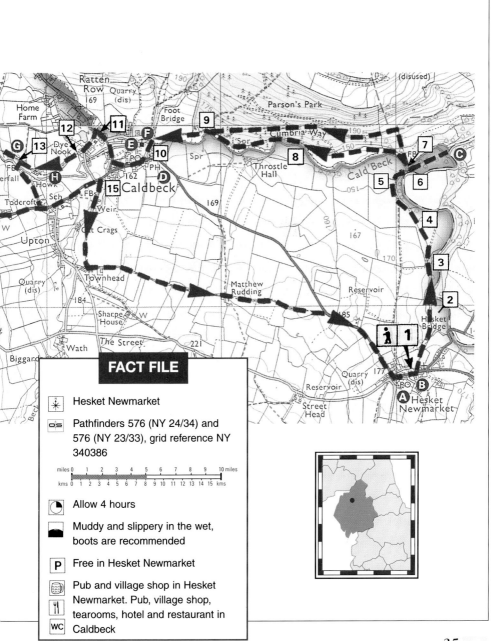

FACT FILE

Hesket Newmarket

Pathfinders 576 (NY 24/34) and 576 (NY 23/33), grid reference NY 340386

miles 0 1 2 3 4 5 6 7 8 9 10 miles
kms 0 1 2 3 4 5 6 7 8 9 10 11 12 13 14 15 kms

Allow 4 hours

Muddy and slippery in the wet, boots are recommended

P Free in Hesket Newmarket

Pub and village shop in Hesket Newmarket. Pub, village shop, tearooms, hotel and restaurant in Caldbeck

35

John Peel

A legend in his own lifetime, John Peel's fox-hunting exploits live on in song.

Everybody knows the song about John Peel, who was born in Caldbeck, but what do we know about the man?

He was a rumbustious fellow who is not remembered as ever having done anything but hunt and drink. As a young man he eloped to Gretna Green with a girl called Mary White, but her family forgave them and her mother endowed her daughter with land that brought an income of about £500 a year.

This was enough for John Peel to be able to indulge himself full time in his passion for hunting. In the field he mixed with men above him in social standing, but he was accepted as the best huntsman of them all.

He became a local legend, credited with setting out at dawn and riding many miles each day – hunting in those parts was both on foot and mounted on horseback. Peel's livery was a grey coat, as it says in the song (which was written by a local man called John Woodcock Graves).

John Peel died in 1854 at the age of 78, after falling off his horse, and is buried in Caldbeck churchyard.

East and West of Eden

Visit an ancient forest on the wooded banks of the Vale of Eden

A statue of Admiral Lord Nelson, above steps leading to the River Eden.

Corby Castle **A** sits above the River Eden at the top of an escarpment. Some parts of it date from the 14th century, but most of it was built about 1810. It is not open to the public.

The walk starts on a gently sloping track through woods. (This is a detour that may be closed. Check on arrival, and if necessary start walk at stage 4.) After about 1/2

mile (800m), you come to the river, by old fish traps and a salmon leap. These were built by monks of the Priory over the river.

The traps mark a turning point back to view an architectural oddity, a statue of Nelson, at the foot of a cascade – an elaborate means of allowing rainwater to drain off the castle estate. A steep path and steps lead back to the castle grounds.

Continued on p. 40➡

37

THE WALK

GREAT CORBY–WETHERAL
Start from village of Great Corby (near castle entrance at point I to check if first part of walk is open to public, otherwise at point 4).

1 (First part of walk may be closed. Check before starting. If closed, start at point 4.) An arrow by the coin box indicates start of the walk. Follow the path along the front lawn, into woods above river. Continue ahead, downhill to the riverbank by the fish traps and salmon leap **B**.

2 Turn right along green walk by river to cascade **C** and caves.

3 Retrace your steps 100 yards (90m) back along river bank, then take steep path on left to top of cascade. At the grass above the summerhouse, turn sharp right to rejoin original path. Bear right to reach the lodge gate.

4 Walk north through the village of Great Corby. Continue ahead, and cross the line at the railway crossing.

5 Turn left to cross the viaduct **D** by the footway beside the railway line. At Wetheral Station, cross over to the opposite platform, using the footbridge.

6 Go through the station yard, then down the steep path and steps, which turn under the viaduct. Turn right along Low Road, to walk with the river on your left. At the end of the road, turn left and go down some steps that lead to the water's edge.

7 Turn right along the river bank to follow a well-trodden footpath to a kissing-gate at the entrance to Wetheral Woods **E**. As you walk you will see to your right the cascade **V** and caves, as well as the statue of Nelson, on the opposite bank of the river. Continue ahead, always bearing left at forks, to St

Constantine's Cells **F**. Retrace your steps a short distance, to where there are some steps on your left. At the top of six steps you will come to a higher path. Turn right.

8 Follow the path, and make for a stile into a field. Follow a line of oak trees to a gate onto a lane.

9 Turn right and follow the lane past the Priory Gatehouse **G** towards the village. At a T-junction, turn right then soon left to visit the church **H**.

10 Retrace steps up the hill. Follow road along side of the green, exiting at far right-hand corner. Right down a lane, past Crown Hotel to station. Cross the footbridge and viaduct to Great Corby, and retrace your earlier steps to return to start of the walk.

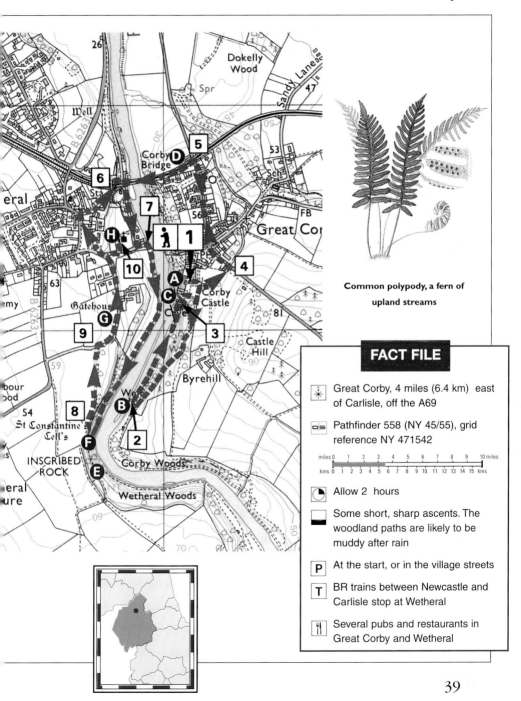

Common polypody, a fern of
upland streams

FACT FILE

❋ Great Corby, 4 miles (6.4 km) east
of Carlisle, off the A69

os Pathfinder 558 (NY 45/55), grid
reference NY 471542

miles 0 1 2 3 4 5 6 7 8 9 10 miles
kms 0 1 2 3 4 5 6 7 8 9 10 11 12 13 14 15 kms

◗ Allow 2 hours

▬ Some short, sharp ascents. The
woodland paths are likely to be
muddy after rain

P At the start, or in the village streets

T BR trains between Newcastle and
Carlisle stop at Wetheral

🍴 Several pubs and restaurants in
Great Corby and Wetheral

The walk leads out of the grounds and through the village of Great Corby to Corby Bridge **D**, a railway viaduct across the Eden. Running alongside the railway line leading to Wetheral station and village is a wooden footpath, which affords a good view downstream. From the station yard, there are steep steps, made from stone sleepers, leading to the river.

As you follow the west bank of the Eden south from the village, the river runs fast and shallow over flat rocks. If you step out (carefully) from the shore onto some of the stone slabs, you get views of Corby Castle, crowning a bend in the river, and the arches of the viaduct, which was built of local sandstone in 1830.

The route passes through a kissing-gate and enters Wetheral Woods **E**. Pied flycatchers and

Tansy grows by the River Eden. It flowers from July to September.

wood warblers inhabit this ancient forest, and water voles and mink have made their homes in the banks. By the path are Himalayan balsam and wild tansy, while willow and alder grow by the water.

The path leads to a series of square-cut caves, hanging high in the sandstone cliff above the river and heavily incised with old graffiti. They are known as St Constantine's Cells **F**, or Wetheral's Safeguards. The saint's connection with them is dubious. Little is known of his life; he may have been either a 6th-century prince or a 10th-century king. The other name refers to the habit of Wetheral monks of using the caves to store valuables.

Norman Priory

The way back leaves the riverside for open fields and a lane to the gatehouse **G** of Wetheral Priory, which was founded in 1088. The gatehouse is all that remains, apart from a few bits of wall that are incorporated into Wetheral Priory Farm.

The lane runs into Wetheral near the Church of the Holy Trinity, St Constantine and St Mary **H**. Although many churches in Scotland are dedicated to Constantine, this is the only one in England. It is built in the Early English style, with the addition of a Victorian tower.

Wetheral, a dormitory village for Carlisle, is a sophisticated place with a gourmet restaurant and two first-class hotels. The village's finest features are its great triangular green and the river, which you recross to return to the start of the walk.

Gills and Valleys

By woods and streams through the South Tyne valley

The market town of Alston is the highest in England.

Alston is the highest market town in England, situated amidst the sweeping landscapes of the North Pennines. On this walk there are magnificent views over the South Tyne valley towards the highest Pennine fells. On the way are 18th-century hill farms, which are still in use, ancient drystone walls and fields grazed by hardy sheep. The route crosses a delightful wooded gill, or ravine, and returns along a section of the Pennine Way. In summer, there is a great wealth of interesting flora and upland birds.

Almshouses

From the top of Alston's main street, beside the Methodist chapel **Ⓐ**, a narrow lane leads out of the town between the

Continued on p. 44➡

41

THE WALK

ALSTON–BLEAGATE
The walk starts from the Methodist chapel **Ⓐ** in Alston.

1 Follow the lane between the Swan's Head and the Chapel until it divides behind the Chapel. Take the left fork of the path and follow it to a small road at Fairhill Cottages **Ⓑ**. Turn left, then right and take the rough track to Fairhill Farm **Ⓒ**. Pass a disused quarry **Ⓓ** on the left and continue on towards Annat Walls **Ⓔ**.

2 Continue uphill, go through a gate, and follow a fence on your right alongside a conifer plantation, then cross a stile beside an oak tree. Cross another field with a wall on the right, then go through an opening in wall ahead and follow a fence on your right. Descend into the wooded valley of Nattrass Gill **Ⓕ** and cross the footbridge over a tributary stream. Climb up to a stile leading into fields again. Follow a line of trees to your left across the field ahead to another stile with High Nest **Ⓖ** about 100 yards (90m) away to the right. At the next stile there is a wooden signpost, which points the way back to Alston.

3 Turn left, then right, onto a lane which continues for about 1/2 mile (800m) until you reach Bleagate **Ⓗ**. Cross the farmyard in Bleagate to a gate and stile, and turn right along the Pennine Way. The path now continues through fields and stiles on a well-trodden grassy path to Nattrass Gill, where there is a footbridge **Ⓙ**. Carry on past a plantation on the left. Follow the path above the River South Tyne, with newly planted trees on the steep bank beside the path, and mature woodland further on towards Alston. On the edge of Alston, pass the youth hostel **Ⓚ**. Join a road above the main A689, then climb steps leading to a narrow lane between the hospital and the school. Follow the lane up the hill to the chapel, to return to the starting point of the walk.

Nature Facts

Male

Female

Orange Tip butterfly. You may see this on lady's smock.

Male

Female

Green-veined white butterfly. Often found on hedge-mustard.

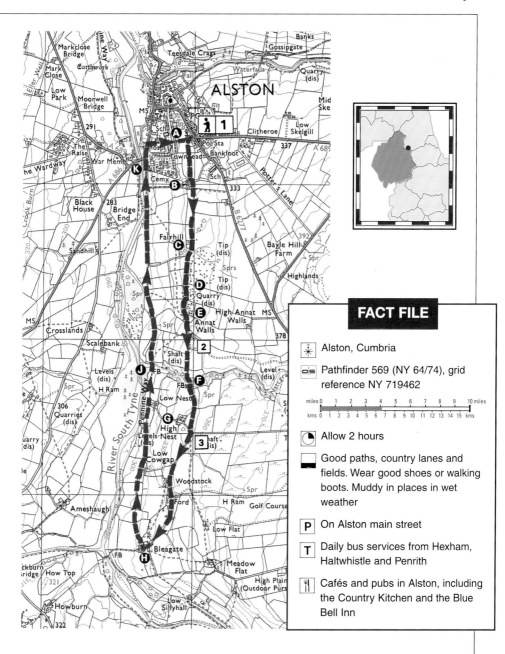

FACT FILE

☀ Alston, Cumbria

▭ Pathfinder 569 (NY 64/74), grid reference NY 719462

miles	0	1	2	3	4	5	6	7	8	9	10 miles
kms	0 1 2 3 4 5 6 7 8 9 10 11 12 13 14 15 kms										

◖ Allow 2 hours

▬ Good paths, country lanes and fields. Wear good shoes or walking boots. Muddy in places in wet weather

P On Alston main street

T Daily bus services from Hexham, Haltwhistle and Penrith

🍴 Cafés and pubs in Alston, including the Country Kitchen and the Blue Bell Inn

drystone walls and a scattering of outlying buildings. The path reaches Fairhill Cottages **B**, which were once almshouses, then follows a track to Fairhill Farm **C**, where there is a barn that has ventilation slits in its side instead of windows.

Annat Walls **E** is another old farm settlement, with fine 18th-century buildings, built from locally quarried limestone, and spring water pouring into a stone well beside the track. The fields here are grazed by sheep, and cut during summer for hay and silage. There are good views of the Penrith road as it climbs towards Hartside Pass, which is often snowbound in winter.

Alston's history is dominated by the development of agriculture and mining in the area. For hundreds of years the mining communities produced lead and silver, and many of the miners managed smallholdings. It was a hard life, and all that remains of those days are old spoil heaps, mineworkings and ruined farmsteads.

The farming life of Alston Moor is still important today, with a quarter of the working population involved in some way with agriculture. Many of the old stone farmsteads have been converted into residential or holiday cottages, and there are

still some small, private coal mines being worked in the area.

The path descends into Nattrass Gill **F**, where there is a lush growth of primroses, cowslips, ferns and mosses. Waterfalls tumble through the sheltered woods of rowan, hazel, sycamore and birch. In the spring there are strong-smelling ramsons (wild garlic), wood sorrel, pansies, lady's mantle, wild raspberries and strawberries, and a variety of ferns.

The footpath climbs steeply out of the gill and back into open country, across fields with clumps of rushes, tiny tormentil flowers and white eyebright. You may see fields planted with coltsfoot. Some of the loveliest yet commonest sights of spring are the tumbling flight displays of the lapwings, with their distinctive 'pee-wit' call.

The route soon joins a quiet lane that leads to Bleagate **D**. This is an old farming settlement, whose name can be found in documents dating from the 13th century. The name means, aptly, 'pasturage for cattle'. Here there is a good view over the valley to the Black Burn. To the south stands the plateau of Cross Fell, which is the highest point in the Pennine area, at 2,930 feet (893m).

Farm buildings constructed in the 18th century, at Annat Walls.

Index